OUR SOLAR SYSTEM

MOONS

by Carolyn Bennett Fraiser

BrightPoint Press

San Diego, CA

© 2023 BrightPoint Press
an imprint of ReferencePoint Press, Inc.
Printed in the United States

For more information, contact:
BrightPoint Press
PO Box 27779
San Diego, CA 92198
www.BrightPointPress.com

ALL RIGHTS RESERVED.

No part of this work covered by the copyright hereon may be reproduced or used in any form or by any means—graphic, electronic, or mechanical, including photocopying, recording, taping, web distribution, or information storage retrieval systems—without the written permission of the publisher.

LIBRARY OF CONGRESS CATALOGING-IN-PUBLICATION DATA

Name: Fraiser, Carolyn Bennett, author.
Title: Moons / by Carolyn Bennett Fraiser.
Description: San Diego, CA: BrightPoint Press, 2023 | Series: Our solar system | Audience: Grades 10–12 | Includes bibliographical references and index.
Identifiers: ISBN 9781678204068 (hardcover) | ISBN 9781678204075 (eBook)
The complete Library of Congress record is available at www.loc.gov.

CONTENTS

AT A GLANCE	4
INTRODUCTION	6
LANDING ON A MYSTERIOUS MOON	
CHAPTER ONE	12
MOONS OF THE TERRESTRIAL PLANETS	
CHAPTER TWO	22
MOONS OF THE GAS GIANTS	
CHAPTER THREE	34
MOONS OF THE ICE GIANTS	
CHAPTER FOUR	46
OTHER MOONS: PLUTO AND BEYOND	
Glossary	58
Source Notes	59
For Further Research	60
Index	62
Image Credits	63
About the Author	64

AT A GLANCE

- Our solar system has more than 200 moons. Scientists believe studying them will help us learn more about our solar system and its history.

- Scientists believe many moons came from leftover gas, dust, and debris when the solar system formed. Other moons were captured asteroids. These moons were pulled into orbit by a planet's gravity.

- The four planets closest to the Sun have very few moons. Scientists think the Sun's gravity prevented more from forming.

- Astronauts from the Apollo missions placed scientific instruments on Earth's Moon. Scientists are still learning more about the Moon and its history.

- Moons can orbit objects besides planets. Scientists have found moons around asteroids and objects in the Kuiper belt.

- Jupiter and Saturn have the most moons of any planets.

- Some moons may contain oceans underneath their crusts. Scientists are eager to explore them to see if life might exist there.

- Several moons show signs of geological activity. This activity has changed landscapes on the moons' surfaces.

- Pluto and its moon Charon are close in size. They are sometimes called a double planetary system. They orbit around each other.

INTRODUCTION

LANDING ON A MYSTERIOUS MOON

Thick orange haze hid the surface of Titan, Saturn's largest moon. No one had ever seen what lay beneath it. That changed in 2005. The *Cassini* spacecraft arrived at the mysterious moon. It released a small probe called *Huygens*. The 700-pound (320 kg) probe fell toward the moon. Then it disappeared into Titan's **atmosphere**.

The *Huygens* probe gathered data as it fell. Scientists back on Earth waited. If the mission succeeded, it would be the first landing in the outer solar system.

Workers prepare to attach the Huygens *probe to the* Cassini *spacecraft.*

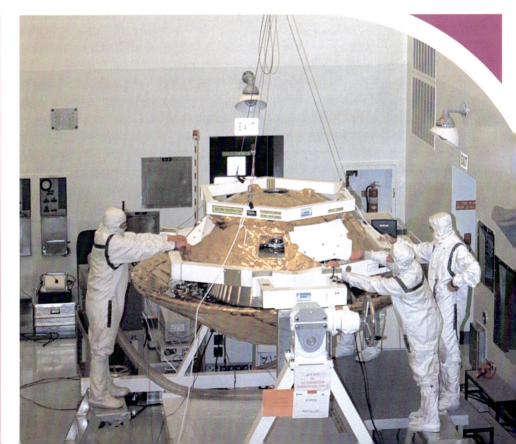

Huygens *touched down softly on the surface of Titan.*

The probe used a parachute to slow down. As it drifted downward, *Huygens* collected photos of a strange world. Titan's surface was not made of rock, but solid ice. The moon had lakes and rivers like those on Earth. But Titan was far too cold for liquid water. Instead, liquid methane flowed through the canyons and fell from the sky like rain. Finally, the probe landed safely. Scientists celebrated the success and got to work studying the incoming data.

THE MOONS OF OUR SOLAR SYSTEM

Our solar system contains more than 200 moons. Each one is unique. Some were once asteroids. Gravity from a nearby planet pulled them into **orbit**. Others formed at the

Scientists are working hard to learn more about the solar system's amazing moons.

same time as the planets. They arose from leftover gas, dust, and debris.

Scientists continue to study these moons. They hope future missions will help us learn about their mysteries. New discoveries may help reveal more about the history of the solar system.

1
MOONS OF THE TERRESTRIAL PLANETS

The four planets closest to the Sun are known as the terrestrial planets. This means they have rocky surfaces. The terrestrial planets have few moons. The Sun's gravity makes it difficult for moons to form and stay in place.

Mercury is the planet closest to the Sun. Venus is next. These are the only two planets in the solar system with no moons. Earth has just one. Mars has two very small moons.

Mercury and Venus, the two planets closest to the Sun, have no moons.

EARTH'S ONE AND ONLY

No moon has been studied more than our own. Scientists have tried to figure out how the Moon formed. The leading idea is called the giant impact **hypothesis**. It says that an object the size of Mars once crashed into Earth. Pieces were knocked into orbit. Over time they joined to become the Moon.

EARTH'S TEMPORARY MOONS

In 2020, astronomers discovered a tiny asteroid orbiting Earth. A few months later, the Sun's gravity pulled it away. Scientists believe that Earth always has at least one of these temporary moons. Most are only a few feet wide.

Some areas of the moon are dark and smooth, while others have many craters.

Later collisions with space rocks left many **craters** on the Moon's surface. High mountains look light gray from Earth. Flat regions are darker. These are called lunar maria. Scientists think lava once flowed across the maria, making them smooth.

The Moon is tidally locked with Earth. This means that the same side always faces Earth. Earth's gravity causes the Moon to spin on its axis at the same speed that it orbits.

The Moon's gravity also pulls on Earth. It creates ocean tides. It slows Earth's rotation by a fraction of a second per year. Scientist Daniel MacMillan says, "The solar day is gradually getting longer because Earth's rotation is slowing down ever so slightly."[1] Sometimes an extra second is added to the calendar to make up for the slowing rotation.

Astronaut Buzz Aldrin climbs out of the lunar lander during the Apollo 11 mission.

In July 1969, American astronauts on the Apollo 11 mission made the first Moon landing. Neil Armstrong and Buzz Aldrin became the first humans to walk on the Moon. They gathered Moon rocks and soil samples. They set up scientific experiments. The astronauts returned safely to Earth.

Five more Moon landings followed. A total of twelve astronauts walked on the lunar surface. The later missions gathered more samples. They brought more advanced gear. The final three missions even brought a lunar rover. This small car let astronauts travel farther from their lander. They could explore a wider area.

The last Apollo Moon landing was in 1972. By 2022, no one had been back to the Moon. But new missions were being planned. In the 2020s, the goal of the US Artemis program was to land more astronauts on the Moon.

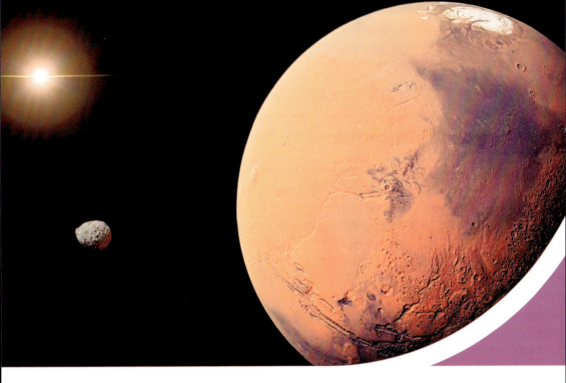

Phobos is small and has an unusual shape.

THE TWIN MOONS OF MARS

Mars only has two moons, Phobos and Deimos. Their names come from Ancient Greek. Phobos means "fear" and Deimos means "terror." They are among the smallest moons in the solar system.

Scientists believe Mars pulled them into orbit from the nearby asteroid belt.

Both moons are covered with craters. They look like lumpy potatoes. Deimos is only 9 miles (15 km) across on its longest side. It takes 30 hours to orbit Mars once. Phobos is about 17 miles (27 km) across at its widest. It is also closer to Mars. It whizzes around the planet in about 7.5 hours.

In fact, Phobos orbits closer than any other moon to its planet. It is just 3,700 miles (6,000 km) from Mars. Every century, it moves 6.6 feet (2 m) closer.

Phobos has many long grooves on its surface. Scientists used to think they were related to a large crater on the moon. But scientist Terry Hurford says new studies tell a different story. Phobos may be breaking apart. He says, "We think that Phobos has already started to fail. The first sign . . . is the production of these grooves."[2]

THE ASTEROID BELT

The asteroid belt is a ring of rocks that orbits the Sun between Mars and Jupiter. There are millions of asteroids in the belt. Scientists believe these asteroids are leftover pieces from the formation of the solar system.

2

MOONS OF THE GAS GIANTS

Jupiter and Saturn are known as the gas giants. These huge planets are made up of colorful, swirling gases. They have no surfaces to land on. But they have rocky moons. These could be places for future missions to land.

The gas giants have many moons. Jupiter and Saturn each have more confirmed moons than all other planets combined. Astronomers expect to discover even more in the future.

Jupiter and Saturn have a few big moons and a large collection of smaller ones.

JUPITER'S MOONS

Jupiter has seventy-nine known moons. This includes fifty-three confirmed moons and twenty-six provisional ones. Confirmed moons have strong evidence supporting their discovery. Provisional ones need more observation to be confirmed. Moons usually get names once they are confirmed.

The four largest are known as Galilean moons. Galileo Galilei discovered them in 1610. Three are bigger than Earth's Moon. They all circle Jupiter on the same plane as its equator. The massive planet's gravity locks them in place.

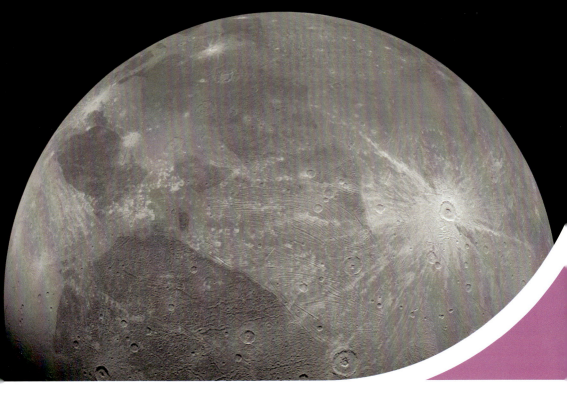

NASA combined multiple photos from the Juno spacecraft to create a sharp view of Ganymede.

Ganymede is the largest moon in the solar system. It's even larger than Mercury. Ganymede has many craters. But other areas are smooth. Water could have once flowed and refrozen on its surface.

Callisto is Jupiter's second largest moon. It is the most heavily cratered object in the solar system. It may have a salty ocean below its surface.

More than 400 volcanoes erupt on the moon Io. They spew rock and gas into space. Gravity from Jupiter and Ganymede pull and squeeze this moon from opposite directions. Lava flows constantly.

Smooth, bright ice covers Jupiter's moon Europa. Reddish-brown cracks crisscross its surface. Scientists believe that under the icy crust lies a global ocean. It could hold more water than the entire Earth. But reaching it would be difficult. A spacecraft would have to drill through miles of solid ice.

This artist's image shows what scientists think the inside of Europa may look like.

Jupiter has dozens of other moons. But they are much smaller than the Galilean moons. The smallest Galilean moon is Europa, at about 1,940 miles (3,100 km) across. The biggest non-Galilean moon is Amalthea. It is about 100 miles (160 km) across. Most of Jupiter's moons are even smaller. Many are just a few miles across.

Amalthea is too small for its gravity to pull it into a round shape. It has a lumpy shape with craters and hills. Amalthea was the fifth moon of Jupiter to be discovered. American astronomer Edward Emerson Bernard found it in 1892.

SATURN'S MOONS

Saturn is famous for its rings, but it also has many moons. It has eighty-two known moons. This includes fifty-three confirmed moons and twenty-nine provisional ones.

The largest of Saturn's moons is Titan. It is about one and a half times the size of Earth's Moon. It is the only moon with a thick atmosphere. In 2005, the *Huygens* probe flew through Titan's orange haze. Cameras and sensors revealed lakes, rivers, and canyons flowing with liquid methane. The methane even evaporates and falls like rain.

SHEPHERD MOONS AND THE RINGS OF SATURN

Several of Saturn's moons are shepherd moons. These moons orbit in the gaps between the rings. Their gravity keeps debris and dust in the rings from straying into space.

This artist's view of Titan's surface is based on data from the Cassini spacecraft.

A new mission to Titan is planned to arrive in the 2030s. NASA will send a drone called *Dragonfly* to the moon. *Dragonfly* will be the size of a small car. It will use propellers to take off, fly around, and land. This will help scientists gather data from several places on Titan. The gravity on Titan is low, and the atmosphere is thick. This will make flying easier than on Earth.

Another of Saturn's large moons is Enceladus. This moon may have a global ocean under its crust. The *Cassini* spacecraft saw a geyser near Enceladus's south pole. The geyser spews water, ice, salt, and carbon compounds into Saturn's rings.

Luciano less was a *Cassini* team member. He was excited about finding water on moons. He says, "The search for water is an important goal in solar system exploration, and now we've spotted another place where it is abundant."[3]

Saturn's smallest moons have many unique features. Epimetheus and Janus switch orbits every four years. Mimas has a huge crater 80 miles (130 km) wide.

LIFE ON MOONS

Scientists hope to study the oceans on Europa and Enceladus. Some of the substances that could support life, including water, have already been found on these icy moons. Scientist Torrence Johnson says, "It's exciting to find another place where we might have liquid water."

Quoted in Tony Philipps, "Callisto Makes a Big Splash," NASA, June 18, 2018. https://science.nasa.gov.

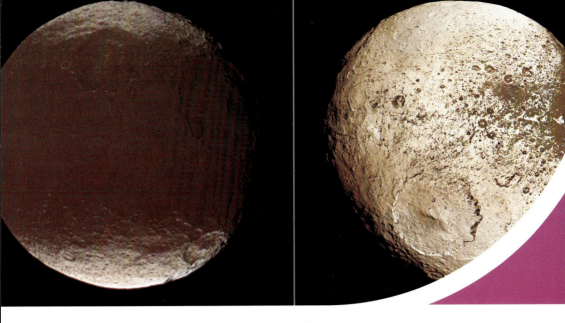

The unusual Iapetus has one light side and one dark side.

It makes the moon look similar to the Death Star in *Star Wars*. The equator of the tiny moon Pan bulges outward. Hyperion has so many craters, it looks like a sponge. The moon Iapetus has one light side and one dark side. Scientists are not sure why.

3

MOONS OF THE ICE GIANTS

Uranus and Neptune are often grouped with the gas giants. However, they have some important differences from the other gas giants. They are smaller and colder than Jupiter and Saturn. They have more slushy ice than flowing gas. For this reason, they are known as the ice giants.

Like the gas giants, the ice giants have many moons. There are twenty-seven orbiting Uranus. Neptune has fourteen. Both planets have rings, though they are not as large as Saturn's. Some of their moons

Uranus (left) and Neptune (right) have many moons, though not as many as the larger Jupiter and Saturn.

act as shepherd moons. Their gravity keeps dust and debris in the rings. Very little is known about these small moons.

THE MOONS OF URANUS

Uranus orbits the Sun on its side. Its moons circle the planet's equator in sideways orbits. This means that several face the Sun with little shadow from the planet.

VOYAGER 2

Voyager 2 launched on August 20, 1977. The probe flew by Jupiter, Saturn, Uranus, and Neptune. *Voyager 2* made new discoveries on its journey. It discovered several moons.

Two of Uranus's moons were discovered in 1787. Two more were found in the 1850s. Astronomer Gerard Kuiper found a fifth in 1948. When the *Voyager 2* spacecraft flew past Uranus in 1986, it found ten more.

Most of Uranus's moons are made of ice and rock. They range from 1,000 miles (160 km) to just 12 miles (20 km) across. The smallest moons are darker than asphalt. Scientists believe they came from an area of icy objects in the outer solar system. This area is called the Kuiper belt. The objects may have been captured by Uranus's gravity.

Titania is Uranus's largest moon and the eighth-largest moon in the solar system.

Many of Uranus's moons are named for characters in plays by William Shakespeare. This includes Titania and Oberon, the largest moons. Craters cover Oberon's crust. One of its mountains rises almost

4 miles (6 km). Scientists think that Titania might be younger. It has fewer craters. But giant canyons scar its surface.

Ariel and Umbriel are the next largest moons. They are close in size. But they are very different from one another. Ariel's surface is bright and smooth. Umbriel is dark with many large craters. A mysterious

THE FRANKENSTEIN MOON

Uranus's moon Miranda is sometimes called the Frankenstein moon. Mismatched rock and jagged cliffs cut across its surface like scars. One ridge drops more than 6 miles (9.7 km). That's five times deeper than the Grand Canyon.

ring 90 miles (140 km) wide glows on one of its sides.

Scientists believe several of these moons could have water underneath their crusts. Scientist Richard Cartwright sees value in studying these moons. He says, "These moons are strange worlds and studying them has the potential for new insight into how geologic processes operate on icy moons."[4]

THE MOONS OF NEPTUNE

Neptune is the most distant planet from the Sun. This makes the planet and its moons

A combination of images from Voyager 2 shows Neptune rising above the horizon on Triton.

very cold. Its largest moon, Triton, is one of the coldest places in the solar system. Temperatures plunge to -391°F (-235°C). Frozen nitrogen covers its crust. Triton is **geologically active**. *Voyager 2* found a geyser on its polar cap. It spews nitrogen into space.

Triton travels in the opposite direction of Neptune's rotation. This is called a retrograde orbit. It is the only major moon to do this. Scientists believe Neptune's gravity may have pulled Triton from the Kuiper belt.

Neptune was the Roman god of the sea. Its moons are named for other sea gods. For example, Triton was a Greek god of the ocean.

Neptune's moons Naiad and Thalassa orbit very close together. But they move at different speeds. Naiad's orbit zigs and

Voyager 2 captured detailed pictures of Triton's landscapes.

zags in a wavelike pattern as it passes Thalassa. Scientist Marina Brozovic says the two moons look like they are dancing. She says, "There are many different types of

THE LARGEST MOONS

These are the seven largest moons in the solar system. Four of them belong to Jupiter. Saturn, Neptune, and Earth have one each.

'dances' that planets, moons, and asteroids can follow, but this one has never been seen before."[5]

Nereid is one of Neptune's outermost moons. It has a very stretched-out orbit. At its closest, it is 840,000 miles (1.35 million km) from Neptune. It gets as far away as 5.98 million miles (9.62 million km). Scientists think it may eventually collide with another Neptunian moon.

4
OTHER MOONS: PLUTO AND BEYOND

Planets aren't the only objects in space with moons. The solar system is also home to dwarf planets and asteroids. Dwarf planets are smaller than planets. Unlike planets, they are too small for their gravity to clear other objects from their orbits. Asteroids are even smaller. These rocky bodies orbit the Sun. Many are located in the asteroid belt.

PLUTO AND ITS MOONS

Pluto was discovered in 1930. For many years, it was considered the ninth planet. Pluto was the smallest planet in the solar

Pluto is the most well-known dwarf planet. Even small objects like this can have moons.

system. It was also the most distant from the Sun. But Pluto's status changed in 2006. Scientists decided to stop classifying it as a planet. Instead, it was a dwarf planet. It is located in the Kuiper belt.

Pluto has five confirmed moons. Scientists think Pluto once collided with another object. Its moons formed from leftover debris.

The largest of Pluto's moons is called Charon. It was discovered in 1978. It's about half the size of the Pluto. No other moon is this close in size to its planet. The remaining four moons are much smaller

The New Horizons probe visited Pluto and Charon in 2015.

than Charon. They are called Nix, Hydra, Kerberos, and Styx. They were discovered in 2005 or later.

Because Charon and Pluto are close in size, they are sometimes considered a double planetary system. They rotate around each other in 6.4 days. Each is tidally locked with the other.

Only one probe has studied Pluto and its moons. *New Horizons* left Earth in 2006. It finally arrived at Pluto in 2015. It captured images of a canyon 1,000 miles (1,600 km) across on Charon's surface. Team member Paul Schenk explains one theory about it. He says, "An internal water ocean could have frozen long ago, and [this] could have led to Charon cracking open, allowing water-based lavas to reach the surface."[6]

New Horizons took sharp photos of Pluto and Charon. But the probe flew past the

New Horizons *took photos of Charon as it flew by. This image collects the sharpest pictures the probe took of the moon's different sides.*

Pluto system quickly. It did not have enough fuel to slow down. It had limited time to study the dwarf planet's small moons. The best pictures of Hydra and Styx are small and blurry.

THE ASTEROID MOONS

In 1993, the *Galileo* probe was headed to Jupiter. On the way, it flew past the asteroid Ida. This small body is in the asteroid belt. It is about 35 miles (56 km) long. *Galileo* took photos of the asteroid.

When scientists studied the photos, they discovered something new. A tiny moon orbited around Ida. The moon was just about 1 mile (1.6 km) wide. They named it Dactyl.

Scientist Torrence Johnson explains that the discovery was not a complete surprise. He says, "It was previously thought that

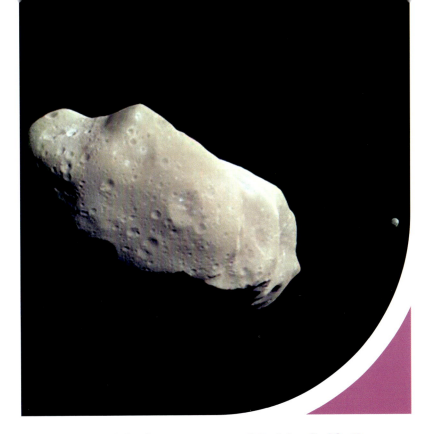

Dactyl (right) is tiny compared to Ida (left), the asteroid it orbits.

natural satellites of asteroids could form, but they probably weren't common." However, Dactyl was still an exciting find. Johnson explains, "Having found one fairly quickly, we can say that they're probably more common than previously thought."[7]

A few years later, a researcher observed a small **moonlet** orbiting another asteroid. The asteroid Didymos orbits just beyond Mars. It is about 0.5 miles (0.78 km) wide. Its moonlet is named Dimorphos. It is about 525 feet (160 m) across.

DART

A mission called the Double Asteroid Redirection Test (DART) launched in 2021. It headed for Didymos. The mission would test if a spacecraft could change the course of an asteroid. This could someday protect Earth from an asteroid strike. DART would run into Dimorphos. Then scientists would watch how the moonlet's path changed.

NASA planned to fly a spacecraft into Dimorphos. They wanted to see if they could change the moonlet's orbit.

MOONS OF OTHER DWARF PLANETS

Pluto is not the only dwarf planet. Some dwarf planets, such as Ceres, have no moons. But others do.

The dwarf planet Makemake is in the Kuiper belt. A telescope orbiting Earth

This artist's image shows Makemake from its small, unnamed moon.

discovered a moon around it in 2016.

Scientists believe it is just 50 miles (80 km) across. More study is needed before this moon receives an official name.

Haumea is another dwarf planet in the Kuiper belt. It is about as big as Pluto. But it spins so fast that it is not round. It looks egg-shaped. Haumea has two moons. They are named Namaka and Hi'iaka. The dwarf planet and its moons are named for Hawaiian goddesses.

The moons of our solar system have a great deal of variety. Some are large worlds, and others are tiny hunks of rock. They have icy oceans, active volcanoes, and huge canyons. Some may even have the features needed for life. Scientists will continue to study these fascinating places.

GLOSSARY

atmosphere

a layer of gas or gases that surrounds a planet

craters

bowl-shaped holes in the ground created by
meteorite impacts

geologically active

a state in which the rocks and substances that make up the
surface of a moon or planet are in the process of changing

hypothesis

a scientific guess based on the available evidence

moonlet

a very small moon

orbit

a regular, repeating path of one object around another

SOURCE NOTES

CHAPTER ONE: MOONS OF THE TERRESTRIAL PLANETS

1. Quoted in Elizabeth Zubritsky, "NASA Explains Why Clocks Will Get an Extra Second on June 30," *NASA*, June 29, 2012. www.nasa.gov.

2. Quoted in Elizabeth Zubritsky, "Mars' Moon Phobos Is Slowly Falling Apart," *NASA*, November 10, 2015. www.nasa.gov.

CHAPTER TWO: MOONS OF THE GAS GIANTS

3. Quoted in "Titan's Underground Ocean," *NASA Science*, June 28, 2012. https://science.nasa.gov.

CHAPTER THREE: MOONS OF THE ICE GIANTS

4. Quoted in Jamie Carter, "Why We Need to Explore the 'Shakespearean' Ocean Moons of Uranus—And There's No Time to Waste," *Forbes*, August 2, 2021. www.forbes.com.

5. Quoted in Ashley Strickland, "Neptune's Moons Perform a Strange Orbit Dance Around Each Other," *CNN*, November 19, 2019. www.cnn.com.

CHAPTER FOUR: OTHER MOONS: PLUTO AND BEYOND

6. Quoted in "Pluto's Big Moon Charon Reveals a Colorful and Violent History," *NASA*, October 1, 2015. www.nasa.gov.

7. Quoted in "243 Ida," *NASA Solar System Exploration*, June 29, 2021. https://solarsystem.nasa.gov.

FOR FURTHER RESEARCH

BOOKS

Nicholas Faulkner and Erik Gregersen, *The Outer Planets*. New York: Britannica Educational Publishing, 2019.

KS Mitchell, *The Gas Giants: Jupiter, Saturn, Uranus, and Neptune*. San Diego, CA: BrightPoint Press, 2023.

Henrietta Toth, *Robotics in Space*. San Diego, CA: BrightPoint Press, 2023.

INTERNET SOURCES

Bill Andrews, "Moons of Our Solar System: There Are More Than You Think," *Discover Magazine*, July/August 2016. www.discovermagazine.com.

Amy Godfrey, "20 of the Most Amazing Moons in the Solar System," *BBC Science Focus*, n.d., www.sciencefocus.com.

"Saturn's Moons," *European Space Agency*, n.d., https://esa.int.

WEBSITES

Juno
www.missionjuno.swri.edu

The official website of the *Juno* mission to Jupiter includes photos and information about the gas giant and its many moons.

NASA Solar System: Moons
https://solarsystem.nasa.gov/moons

NASA's website features in-depth information about all the moons in the solar system.

New Horizons
http://pluto.jhuapl.edu

The website of the *New Horizons* mission features information about the spacecraft's encounter with Pluto and its moon Charon.

INDEX

Amalthea, 27–28
asteroid belt, 20, 21, 47, 52
asteroids, 9, 14, 21, 44, 46–47,
 52–54

Callisto, 25, 44
Cassini, 6, 31
Charon, 48–50

Deimos, 19–20
dwarf planets, 46, 48, 55, 57

Earth, 9, 13, 14, 16, 26, 31, 54
Enceladus, 31, 32
Europa, 26–27, 32, 44

Galilean moons, 24, 27
Ganymede, 25–26, 44

Haumea, 57
Huygens, 6–9, 29

Io, 26, 44

Jupiter, 21, 23, 24–28, 34, 36, 52

Kuiper belt, 37, 42, 48, 55, 57

life, 32, 57

Makemake, 55–56
Mars, 13, 14, 19–20, 21, 54
Mercury, 13, 25
Miranda, 39
Moon, 14–18, 24
Moon landings, 17–18

Neptune, 34, 35, 36, 40–45

Phobos, 19–21
Pluto, 47–51, 55, 57

rings, 28, 29, 31, 35, 36

Saturn, 6, 22–23, 28–33, 34,
 35, 36
shepherd moons, 29, 36
Sun, 12–13, 14, 21, 36, 40, 47, 48

Titan, 6–9, 29–31, 44
Titania, 38–39
Triton, 41–42, 44

Uranus, 35, 36–39

Venus, 13

IMAGE CREDITS

Cover: © Muratart/Shutterstock Images
5: © Dotted Yeti/Shutterstock Images
7: © KSC/NASA
8: © ESA/JPL/NASA
10: © Dotted Yeti/Shutterstock Images
13: © Vadim Sadovski/Shutterstock Images
15: © Goddard/GSFC/NASA
17: © JSC/NASA
19: © Dotted Yeti/Shutterstock Images
23: © Kirschner/Shutterstock Images
25: © SwRI/MSSS/Kalleheikki Kannisto/JPL-Caltech/NASA
27: © JPL-Caltech/NASA
30: © JPL/NASA
33: © Space Science Institute/JPL/NASA
35: © Tristan 3D/Shutterstock Images
38: © JPL/NASA
41: © USGS/JPL/NASA
43: © JPL/NASA/Wikimedia
44: © Mark Garlick/Science Source
47: © Buradaki/Shutterstock Images
49: © Diego Barucco/Shutterstock Images
51: © JHUAPL/SwRI/NASA/Wikimedia
53: © JPL/NASA
55: © Johns Hopkins APL/NASA
56: © John R. Foster/Science Source

ABOUT THE AUTHOR

Carolyn Bennett Frasier grew up just south of Kennedy Space Center in Florida and was fascinated with the Moon and stars. A former journalist, she loves to write about space, nature, and stories buried in history. She currently lives in Brevard, North Carolina, where she works as a graphic designer for nonprofit organizations and mentors teens who love to write.